OZ

Books by Nancy Eimers

Oz
A Grammar to Waking
No Moon
Destroying Angel

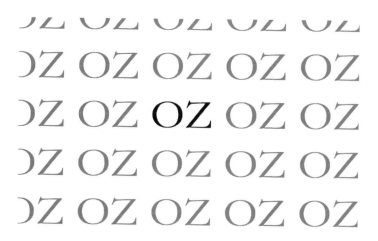

poems by

Nancy Eimers

Carnegie Mellon University Press
Pittsburgh 2011

Acknowledgments

Grateful acknowledgment is made to the editors of the following journals in which these poems appeared, sometimes in different versions:

5 AM: "Flicker"
Barrow Street: "The Small Hours"
Dunes Review: "Address to a Stack of My Journals, "Future Parking Lot," "The Cold War Special: Tin Litho Dollhouse with Bomb Shelter, 1962"
Field: "Bird Nests over the Gates to Terezín," "White-throated Sparrow"
Fifth Wednesday: "All the Toys Are Vanishing," "Confession of a Luddite," "Julie's Mouth"
Grist: "Couplets: On a Mowed Lawn," "To a Friend Whose Mother May Be Dying"
Laurel Review: "Grassland," "The Pinwheel in Our Neighbors' Flowerbed"
Mentor & Muse: Essays from Poets to Poets: "Book of Invisible Things"
New Ohio Review: "Glacier," "Y at the End of It"
Parthenon West: "Pelicans, in a Time of War"
Poetry Miscellany: "Long Gone Conversation about Cancer"
three candles: "El Rancho," "Lost Continent"
Triquarterly: "Crawl Key Wind," "Fifth of July," "My Parents Contemplate Moving a Last Time"
West Branch: "Afterlives," "September Rain"
Zone 3: "Derby Winner Clings to Chances for Recovery," "How We Thought about Toys," "Infant Sight, or Thirty-Four Lines Set Adrift," "On Not Talking Politics with My Sister," "Reading the Ice," "Trapped Miners 'May Not Be Found,'" "You Are Hereby Notified"

Heartfelt thanks to Betsy Sholl for counsel and encouragement with this collection, and to my mother and father, my sister and brother, Daneen Wardrop, Gloria Simmons, Jim Ferreira, Mary Ruefle, David Wojahn, Rich Lyons, and Beckian Goldberg for their abiding support. To Bill, all the love and gratitude there is.

This work was supported by funds from the Faculty Research and Creative Activities Support Fund, Western Michigan University.

Book Design: Anh Bui

Library of Congress Control Number 2010928355
ISBN 978-0-88748-532-9

10 9 8 7 6 5 4 3 2 1

Contents

for Bill, and for Mom

I

Grassland

There is something furtive about the water here.

It is most itself at dawn or dusk.
It falls in a haze,

it speaks to the grass in a whisper.

But the outgoing, voluble grass

fills in gaps in the conversation.
There are citizens who attend to it

better than others. Grass refers to itself
or it overflows.

As a matter of policy, all it witnesses
and all you ask

the grass denies:

in the end, every lawn mower
is just a trailing off.

First there were streets and driveways,
then the houses, one by one,

amid the ploughed-up loneliness,

and the people
to come and settle it.

Only then the grass. Around. After, before.

There are over 9,000 species. The terrestrial, not to mention
the aquatic.

Its fruit is dry and dull
on stalks that bend to the shear of wind.

It used to roll and roll without impediment
and say expanse.

On a windless day it still resembles a body of water
but only

once you've closed your eyes.

Oz

Always a woman and her daughter shopping down the mall, never to get to the end of their sentences, under skylights, hanging baskets, petunias, air ferns, dieffenbachia, through the food court echoing like an indoor pool, past the carousel, up and down escalators, around the island of coin-operated vibrating easy chairs, out of one store into another, down the aisles, into the dressing room, where one of them, the daughter, usually, steps out of her clothes

*

alluring   the loneliness thus brought to earth   she trying on her body in the mirror

*

while the other, the mother, her arms full of garments, is out there looking high and low for more, to be fit over the head or shrugged into or pulled up to the waist, to be buttoned or belted or zipped or tied or left open to fall in the most beautiful folds—

*

In a dressing room there is waiting, there is repose, there is quietude, peace, there is ease, unease, you can sit on the bench or you can loll, you can settle, you can while away time, you can look at your watch and tap your foot, you can hum, you can steep, is she ever coming back, can you even remember what she looks like, is her hair wren-brown or white as snow, do you look like her, did she ever look like you, will her face have aged, when will you have exhausted her?

*

Frock, gown, raiment, covering, apparel, attire, habiliment, costume, gaudery, frippery, call it what you will, the body needs it, hands need gloves, eyes need sunglasses, paired and hung on revolving racks, teenagers hug themselves, waiting in line to be pierced with silver and gold, earlobes and brows and noses and lips, how much will it hurt, will it burn, will it be cold, and what of the piercing of the tongue?

*

13

If things can be said to wait, then mannequins wait, the ones without heads, the ones with steel or gold-painted knobs for heads, the bald, the Bendies, the torso forms, the ones without arms, the ones without legs, the "abstract" ones with oblong, featureless heads, the ones in Victoria's Secret whose faces—they mostly don't have faces these days—look stunned or remote or imperturbable. If they have hands the fingers are webbed, or if they are not, as window dressers know, you must take care as the fingertips break off easily. If things can be said to wait, they wait for a bus, wait up at night and wait for the wagon, wait just a minute and stall and hope against hope and tarry hopelessly.

*

L. Frank Baum, author of *The Wizard of Oz*, also a retail art director, dreamed up the idea that shops should be grand enough to intimidate shoppers, so they, so you and I would find ourselves unnerved and grope to speak with cash, in our hands, in your hands and mine those loose unending sentences. . . .

*

Mirrors compressing us, occasions rehearsing us, wedding dresses, dress for the bridesmaid, mother of the bride, cruise glitterati, control top panties and panty hose shaping us, you, my mother, launching me into each dress, *just try it, you never know till you put it on*, hope as it ever will be, you and I as we never were, my body a ship smacking into the lifted bottle—my body the Empire State Building, the Palfy Palace, McDonald's arches, a flying buttress, a pyramid—

*

What to do with you now, sense of presence, you someone there just out of sight, over the shoulder, beyond the corner of the eye, on the other side of the curtain, my body having been shaken out of its clothes, alone and waiting on the bench for you, the mirror conducting its inquisitions, how long has it been, what did she say, did she say bide or was it abide, how long did she say to wait and for what and was she a prophet then, did she miss me, did she did each of us have even then some sense of an end just out of sight, what time was it when waiting first began to change into grief inside this dressing room where nothing will be remembered years later or even, at the time, be ready to explain itself. . . .

14

Future Parking Lot

Who will the parkers be? Who their passengers?

Why will they park here? In the space of an average lifetime, how long will they have stayed? Where will they go after this?

Assuming the summers will be hot, will a store ever be thought of as a river? How long and hot and troubled must the day have been?

What signs, markers, attendants, portents, comets, billboards, dust motes, tremblings will drive them here?

Does direction dissipate in a parking lot? What winds will blow over this place?

Assuming the winters will be long, how bleak a light is required for the lot to be full? Half full? Will it ever, ever be empty?

Silence the streets cast off. Motions the tires disown. How will the parkers weather arrivals? Departures? Each other's? Their own?

Getting out of their cars, at what velocity will the parkers be walking and what oh what will they be walking towards? Hands in their pockets, hands swinging in the air. Holding hands. Every hand with its parking space.

How much more than its space will each car devour?

Parking during a time of rapid change, during war, while in love, after sex, before sex, without sex, verging on divorce, the hour before marrying, in an election year, after therapy, chatty, without words, will the immersion be short- or long-term?

How long will each parking space have to wait? Must waiting, then, have an object?

How small a dark resides beneath each car at noon on the sunniest day? How still a marsh will not resume in the night?

How high up will space have to go, after this?

Infant Sight, or Thirty-four Lines Set Adrift

we seem to want something

—

from a dark that has never

—

been outside   from a stillness so charged

—

it is as a living body   as once

—

in a tinderbox cathedral's dark

—

I saw a plaster statue of a dead man

—

sit up   arms crossed   in its coffin of glass

—

I blinked   it was lying down

—

no one else had seen   in the blink of an eye

—

my eye   it had laid itself back down

—

inside a sleep

—

composed of gypsum   water   sand   and sometimes hair

—

I was nine   Nogales   Mexico

—

was I don't know how

—

careworn a town   now   here

—

a crowd of us turns our faces

—

up to the Infant of Prague   a

—

small wax child   a stillness

—

unchildlike   so profound it almost promises

—

to move   brow   lip   tearless eye

—

dear emptiness   we in our childishness

—

that never plays

—

look up at a never-never

—

boy looking out over our heads

—

its only family a family of candles

—

tapers   votives   flickers   gutterings

—

under the maybe-

—

yes-maybe-no of the candleflames

—

under the lifted brows   the polite

—

impasse of a face

—

each living body's stir and drift

18

—

is the angry orphan here

—

whose heart-thumping on-and-on

—

the dark is too polite to hear

Long Gone Conversation about Cancer

—for Julie

That certain dark of a parking lot
not going anywhere: yeah we have to go
and maybe there's even
a future awaiting each of us like two tin cans

on the ends of a string,
maybe we're both worried soon there won't be anything
rippling in the string
but we stay a little while.

Talk is not a spotlight. It is not a car
with a single headlight. It is
not a silver slipper kicked off
though the moon is all of these.

Up above somewhere are a million stars
but they aren't available just now
too busy being outshone
and gone. But maybe

it's OK, as long as moonlight shines
on the garbage cans and it escorts
a woman talking on a cellphone
safely through the silences of cars,

as long as kids on skateboards surf forever
up the concrete steps
like movies playing backwards
you and I might just keep standing here

after class
before the night ahead,
your mouth drawn to the side
as if just saying were pulling the string,

the rest of everything just wait & see
whatever that may do to you—
how late inside—
that takes some getting used to—

20

Derby Winner Clings to Chances for Recovery

—Barbaro, summer 2006

The paper says it has a fifty-fifty chance.
Only yesterday we were talking about numbers.
Difference between fifty and 50
and the place each one arrives in the brain.

A horse can count but horses do not know arithmetic.
It taps a foot but invisible string is tied
from its brain to the brain of a man
and it lifts a hoof and then between them is

the number three. And pardon me, a horse is not
an it. A horse can break three bones
in the leg and still live, still cling to life, as they say.
A horse can have a fifty-50 chance

but if you tunnel straight down it's another century in horse-history
and I don't know any numbers for that dark.
Just the cupped-hand light of miners' lamps.
But how did they get horses down there

Emile Zola once asked. They lower them as foals and after that
they never come back up. As dray horses
they live and die and they are buried there.
And surely then the notebook in his brain could feel

a horse's being as two fingers might
pinch out a candle flame. Or if not two then 2
and then the problem has a lonely coal-black
finitude. What's a horse who craves his own

unlonely endless space supposed to do? Voices on the radio
can sound like dotted lines between the faintest stars.
A man was saying children get interested early
in math and science, so instruction cannot wait for 12 or 13

to increase the pace to higher math. The mystery of outer space
zoomed into the integers exactly then
in the middle of a sunny afternoon.
At least numbers acknowledge there are things we don't admit

to language. Doesn't static kind of glint, like stars?
It was a marvel. Surgery for hours. Five.
The horse was standing after the surgery.
Fifty, fifty. Long pastern, fetlock, cannon bone. This morning's

front page bore a diagram with dotted lines
from words to broken places in the leg
of Barbaro. Look what all's inside his leg! I thought.
If ever we should speak more brokenly—

if ever we could all just limp along.
On the radio I heard the horse's owner saying she didn't
        question the sport
but neither did she call it a science or an art.
She said you shouldn't fall in love

with your horses, but when it came to Barbaro
she was a foolish woman (with an old man's voice).
If racehorses are more alive
when racing, what do you call a pastern bone so shattered
        even the broken-

hearted surgeon numbers the fragments "20-plus"?
It takes twelve columns for the *OED* to demarcate
four legs and the monumental body over that;
the *Illustrated Oxford* almost gives up

on it, placing words around the horse's body
like a halo, forty-two of them, with arrows pointing to some few
features of a landscape that resides between the flowing mane and tail
unfenced, instinctively remote.

Trapped Miners 'May Not Be Found'

—*headline*, USA Today, *Aug. 20, 2007*

A topic sentence can be found anywhere in a paragraph, but in the dark is there still a controlling idea? Probably everyone speculates but nobody says it out loud though it's in all the papers. I can already feel other sentences yielding to seismic vibrations that could mean the underground presence of nothing or something, additional cave collapse, small earthquake, a beating heart. "May" is softer than "will" but harsher than hawthorn blossoms. The mine's co-owner speaks for himself (and his "co") but this morning some of his words are in a minor key. It's time to modulate. He also says "locate"; he might as well have said *determine or specify the position of.* There's a sense of picking one's way through a proverbial rubble. He could have said *park, stand, pitch, moor, graft.* If he had said *cradle* our hearts would have pounded illegally. The final sentence may restate the controlling idea, are we ready for that? "May" is a kind of permission, a kind of transition to what? *Concern for the future. Forward-looking corporations. Under 2,000 feet of mourning.* For shock value the families' spokesman uses the word "expire." That always sounds to me like a buzzer going off at the end of something. A race, an operation. *The end of something.* Not that sound when a truck is backing up but a harshness, wires shorting out. Process paragraphs have a time element: step one, step two. . . . We tried one thing; then we tried another. Inside *be found* is a grammar of de-emphasis. "May" is a small space, "not" is immensity. To get from one to the other it has to be so dark you can't see a hand in front of your face.

Couplets: On a Mowed Lawn

Walking across it leaves no mark.
Why do I think of snow?

—

This flowing outward too neatly contained.
This vastness not of water but of parking lots.

—

No—close shave—it keeps things close to the vest.
It is not a greeting, it is not even a nod.

—

Velvety from certain distances—across the street—
some unseen blackness softens it.

—

After watching TV quiz shows all afternoon,
that summer sadness and the daylight moon.

—

Once subject to dollar spot, snow mold, fairy rings.
Now subject to chemical burn.

—

Vermeer's *Girl Reading a Letter at an Open Window*,
an antique privacy when the mower stops. . . .

—

If a bit of soil crumbles in the fingers, is it past time
to water it heavily?

—

In certain tricks of light, on baseball fields roller-mowed in stripes, it strobes, it is a vanishing.

September Rain

It is raining everywhere;
                    rain is so monotonous
or is that the mind?
                    For really, morning is manageable
and specific, a series of windows
                    changing like a Quik-Stop
camera trained now
                    on the counter, now on the backs
of customers always impatient
                    to pay, now on the parking lot
where after midnight emptiness
                    sometimes trades itself in
for a car or two.
                    In every scene it is raining
though the cat keeps changing
                    windows as if to find a sunny day
out there. Sometimes her head jerks,
                    tracing the path of whatever
is passing erratically above or below
                    what I can see from here,
bird or squirrel or even the rain
                    slanting sideways, transcribed
by her neck and eye muscles
                    but occurring to me only
as something I will never see
                    or even guess precisely enough
as if my mind were wearing glasses
                    composed entirely of middle distances,
so when I look up from my book
                    everything gets hazy right at the places trees
turn into the possibility
                    there could possibly ever again
be sunlight and, behind it, a night
                    where stars had already begun.

Pelicans, in a Time of War

spring 2004

1. Crawl Key

The pelicans are still as carven things
on the branches of mangroves across the narrow channel.
They have the quality of painted wood,
a something between texture and immobility.
They are stillnesses issuing out of wood.
They are paragraphs, each,
of a restlessness come perfectly
to a branch. Not light,
I want to say come to light
on a branch, but if anything
they come to heavy. To
arrive. They are arrivals,
small boats, each at the end of its trip.
At the end of the day
we say. At the end of the day,
looking back to assess, a they
about to turn and look and gather
into we—

2. Valhalla Point

To wake in the night to a papery rattling
of palms in wind
like low talk in another room
or even night TV—as a child I thought of this
as the "why" kind of talk, all dotted lines,
so far adrift from what it means,
that other room,
the mouths of my parents,
the mouths on TV talking gently for all of us.
It scares me a little,
the Florida wind blowing night and day
great guns
since the day we arrived.

27

3. Bahia Honda State Park

Elizabeth Bishop's palm trees
clatter in the stiff
breeze like the bills of the pelicans.
Four pelicans on the water now
are buoyant as wooden floats. On a piling sits
a fifth one battered softly
by wind
but it doesn't move very much or fall;
to stay in place it adjusts, small motions,
a balancing.

4.

We read no newspapers these days, time has the sound and
            weight of paper
blowing softly at night,
when the rooms of the little motels along the highway
fill up with souls.

And the dead are moved secretly in the night

to bypass our TVs,

only a sound of trucks in our sleep
down the solitary highway on the Keys.

5. Walking Trees

The pelicans look like folk art
carved oak painted white and yellow and gray
by somebody for whom heavy and light-weight
are an abiding contradiction.

For whom the heaviness was not
despondency. No. It was light.

It can squat on a dock and lean,
a compact mass, and maybe fall
to sleep.

Valhalla is so quiet.   Its sound is the wind
that never stops, and the seaweed
shaped like a coconut with a blaring
open mouth

and the mangroves
walking out of their huddle.

Odin was the god of wisdom and war.
For whom there was no contradiction.

6. Cloudy Morning

Nouns—*Warning, caution, notice, caveat, admonition, admonishment, motion,
exhortation; threat, growl; lesson, example; forewarning, foreboding, premonition,
handwriting on the wall, Mother Carey's chicken, storm petrel, bird of ill omen,
gathering clouds*

light through an envelope   light without a source

pearly light

a water lapping back and forth

coral and limestone islands and reefs talking quietly underwater

the patient links in a chain-link fence

7. How We Will Talk about This

things we do in this weather
seem a little unreal   even a little mad
driving to the store   turning left onto the highway
trying to enter the zoom of traffic like trying to speak
rationally to an irrational universe

all this for a newspaper to read one morning

madness at Abu Ghraib   wind bending back
the arms of trees   some words are almost things

we can pass them
off   semantics   words debating words
torture vs. *abuse*   *fraternity prank   just a few*
bad apples the geneva
convention a Republican senator
"outraged at the outrage"

maybe our newspapers should be blank
maybe our folded newspapers   flung at dawn
dream in arcs
of landing bright and mute
maybe our radios should blare out static
to the stars
maybe someone will figure out how to translate rain

8. *Pelecanus occidentalis*

when I take off my glasses

the perching
cormorants on the pilings out there in the water
turn into erratic quotation marks
around nothing

Verbs—speak, say, utter, soliloquize, pronounce, ventriloquize.
Cite, enumerate, itemize, harp on, specify.

Talk to us, harangue us, apostrophize, buttonhole.
Hold forth, recite for us, nasalize.
Give voice to us, comment, greet us, inveigh, negotiate, plead, make noise.

when I put my glasses on
a line of pelicans flies low and away
like some nameless source

away from their breeding grounds
they are silent birds

Crawl Key Wind

Something you knew in your sleep, the wind
had been blowing all night, like news
turned down below its brawn

of words. There were boats in it, and trees blowing sideways,
trucks adrift in their static stretching to Key West
from Miami. Pelicans

hung in the lower branches,
they rocked and were shaken as empty cradles
all the night.

On still nights a moving light across water
had had an object—had been going somewhere,
and going, that was one kind of sorrow.

This had all the lights in it moving, every streetlight
had the reined-in sorrow of a buoy.
If you woke and looked outside and held

still watching, you were carried along and you fell
asleep and wind steered you again
like an island out to sea, and sleep had no object,

being the object, birds flew over it
and the trunks of palms on shore braked on and the fronds
lunged and the souls of newspapers

offered day their rolled-up flight.

Glacier

To watch this losing part of itself—

this frozen dash,
a sign, a pause, a being *poised*—

cliffhanger
at the speed of ice—

just think, says the ranger, it is made of individual *snowflakes*—
I love that bend of her voice
into my head where her sentence goes on—

compressed into a vastness, making this one incredible thing
moved along by the force of its enormous weight,
finding its way down out of the mountains

in the shape of an S—relentless plurality—all those battered
snowflakes—
to the sea.

At one place in its side
three ice-caverns—two eyes and a mouth—so like

—so strange—Munch's *The Scream*.

Each calving's a fusillade—
the sound an "outpouring of anything,"

an *inner* surge.

If there is a waiting, it is ours.
Watching the face change its expression

every time a chunk of ice breaks off—

and yet behind it this *entirety*—boundless, immense, this tidy sum—
the face forlorn—dejected—hangdog now—
our faces turned to it, our eyes and cameras trained on it

as if to document the very moment
something in us changed,
the ship turning in place—deft for so big a thing—

while all along immensity recedes so incrementally we can't—
we just can't
put a human face on it—

II

In it a half-opened door waits and suddenly we're inside.
It is the old human dream of being small enough.

Vivien Greene,
English Dolls' Houses of the Eighteenth and Nineteenth Century

The desperate toys
of children. . . .

William Carlos Williams

All the Toys Are Vanishing

Whether a shoe-doll with a heel for a face or a Polish horse carved of cheese or my whistle-boat or a broomstick horse or a James Bond Pistol Cap with Silencer, all the toys are vanishing. As with tickets, coupons, postcards, airsick bags, there is something see-through about them, either they are the ghosts or we are. A toy is a veil, a toy is a scrim of falling snow, and as with all things that act as curtains, there is the question of what is on the other side. A cradle, a bed, a tree, the bones of the hand, a bird's nest, all of them, nothing? One day we will group them with books and call them ephemera. Oh my friends living far in the future, I am sorry I sat you down on a couch and chastised you for you were innocent without toys. Sometimes a toy will disappear suddenly, sometimes it takes centuries. We can only hope it will find its way back, maybe on the other side of the world, in a hut, in a barn, out on the lawn with the stargazers. A woman, a famous dollhouse collector, left a Victorian dollhouse outside beneath a muddy plastic sheet in order to tend it fastidiously in her mind, even down to the miniscule porcelain teacups on a table made by the plastic piece they put in a pizza box to hold the lid up away from the pizza. In my mind I see toys left out in the snow, I see toys underwater netting glints like riverine dreamcatchers. Seaweed castles with their Ophelian drift are sadder than coral, which is dying out anyway. When I hear the song of the Carolina wren I could break my heart for it speaks as hoarsely as the gears of my childhood music box whose back leg is anchored on by ancient chewing gum. On the lid is painted the picture of a cabin beside what I in my adulthood recognize as a glacier. Passing by so subtly it is out in the open.

The Cold War Special: Tin Litho Dollhouse with Bomb Shelter, 1962

> *... toys helped them ... to pass from a dream world into a real world.*
> *Antonia Frasier,* A History of Toys

In its future strangers will be signaling other strangers on eBay in quest of toy folding cots for the bomb shelter, *which are extremely hard to find. I need one more to complete the set.* All these plaintive messages typed and flying invisibly from one set of fingertips to another—do we own our fingertips?

*

—Hi, I have bought a toy cottage to build. It seems to be overwhelming. The directions scare to me to death.

—Hat shop and contents 90 pounds. Shoe shop with contents 80 pounds. Both 1/12.

—i would love to do a room where mourners have come to pay thier last respect it will be victorian

obvisouly i will need a coffin ect wot else wud i have in the room flowers ect, if any one has any pics or know where to find ideas from i would be very greatful

—I found how to make a wreath to put on the coffin, and how to make a Victorian Coffin Pall.

*

When children play with dollhouses their faces are serious. Is this play? Can we say they are happy when they hold a table or bed or a Frigidaire in the hand, when they peer into rooms they cannot enter, are they entranced—some part of them already gone inside—can we call it sad?

*

They started making dollhouses out of tin so the parents of Cold War girls could afford to buy them and put them under their Christmas trees. Sheet metal upon which was painted: wallpaper, paneling, paintings in frames, mirrors—blank—towels on towel racks, clothes hampers, blackboard and toy soldiers in the baby's room, fireplaces, sometimes with a roaring fire and sometimes with a stack of logs—ah happy happy boughs—never to be lit. In the bomb shelter—1962 only, it replaced the garage—walls upon which were painted: hanging pans and a fire extinguisher, shelves with stacks of canned goods, a radio, folded blankets, a Red Cross kit. Above the meat grinder a hanging calendar. It is May.

*

It was recommended that people stay in the shelter full time for at least fourteen days after a nuclear blast. Families with children were advised to stock their shelter with recreational materials to break the monotony. Monopoly games were popular. Other suggested items included playing cards and diaries to keep a record of one's stay.

*

In the 17th century a woman in Amsterdam put thirty thousand guilders into the restoration and furnishing of her dollhouse—more than the cost of one of the actual merchant houses along the canals. You can see it today in the Rijksmuseum. Mrs. Graham Greene, who began collecting dollhouses during the Blitz, would later curate the Rotunda dollhouse museum, lavish addition to her home. She would not allow children to enter the museum.

*

1962. Neptune and Pluto align. Ranger III misses the moon by twenty-two thousand miles. Everyone is anxious though most of us don't know there is a rocket up there observing the invisible X-rays over the atmosphere. Cargo ships are heading for Cuba. Clouds and stars, in case of nuclear missiles, for fourteen days a child will have to imagine you. Stay calm. Prepare. Have on hand a game of Monopoly, a deck of cards, and a child, *wild beast or angel who is able to pass from one world to another without perceiving any difference.*

*

Dollhouses may have doors of plastic or wood. Dutch doors. Traditional 6-panel doors. You can special-order Victorian doors, swinging doors, French doors, false doors that are sheerly decorative though in Egyptian tombs they functioned as passageways between the living and the dead. Some dollhouse doors have leather hinges. There are hinged dollhouses you can open like doors and lonely, futuristic, open-plan dollhouses with no doors at all, and yet still we are denied, we must grieve from outside, we are lost in thought. *Toys of contemplation*, someone called them.

*

Vivien Greene, her husband staying in London in a place he only later admitted had been his "second establishment"—a home invisible to his wife, address concealed from her lips—used to restore Victorian dollhouses in the long evenings during the blackouts, scraping off old wallpaper with a piece of broken glass.

*

Louis Marx, Toycoon, the Henry Ford of toys, would you also proffer to a child the gift of the first heavy smog over the city of London, 1952? Place the triple-train disaster that year in Tokyo under the Christmas tree, or the Small-Boy test shot in Nevada?

*

Dear Diary, the game of eternity is familiar, a little dull. A room without TV. *Obviously I will need a coffin.*

*

Like a coffin or playing card or a cloud or the Scottie dog in a Monopoly game, this tin dollhouse is a thing, it cannot raise or lower its voice, it is not about language and it is not even mute. It is more like the part of a word that is never pronounced. It need not accuse itself when arraigned. It might be a kindness to place it outside in the moonlight. In dreams it seems to approach, and then it is gone and was never there.

40

Flicker

Flicker in morning seen through opera glasses.
—*Joseph Cornell, in his diary*

Because "distance is the soul of beauty"
you needed small, discreet binoculars
for a bird to pass through the objective lens,
prism, the eyepieces, past the cornea

through the pupil to the sacristy
inside the eye. But the flicker is not a delicate bird.
Red nape, yellow underwing, white rump
and a loud inquire for a call.

Heavy going resistance—work & home—
neurotic fussing Mother—Robert lingering—
then a note about Juan Gris' use of orange and blue.
Does "lingering" mean living on?

Or is this a code for measuring time at home:
to fuss, annoyingly fast; to linger, heartbreakingly slow?
In Gris' *Figure Seated in a Café*
a stripe of blue behaves like a shaft of light would

if the sun were blue.
And the orange planes of a newspaper overlap,
the word *matin* near the center.
Is morning more bearable in French?

There is no living apart. There is reading,
then napping. Working downstairs in the cellar.
Bickford's cafeteria, automat, radio on in the kitchen,
still the touch of the orange.

Face of every cashier and waitress on earth
remote as an empty stadium, a moonless night.
And the beauty of that. *Going into cellar*
after sleep on couch

41

"loneliness is stronger than sex."
There is midnight and two and three and four,
and then there is six in the morning.
Matin. Your presence is required.

Who knows how the day will go?
Beautiful blues / orange,
a toy kangaroo remembered from a department store window
at Christmas, *blowing real soap bubbles.*

There are sea shells, watch parts, miscellaneous
man reading a newspaper in a café,
blue stripe, orange triangle, no face,
maybe later a piece of pie.

Maybe it's raining outside and the damp gets in,
the little automat windows clouding over
until there is nothing
to choose but the invisible.

How We Thought about Toys

In 1943 Joseph Cornell spent eight months working
at a defense plant, testing radio parts.

This is no shooting gallery for children.
Deborah Soloman,
on Cornell's 1943 Habitat for a Shooting Gallery *box*

Somehow out of a factory came these birds.
Out of a nobody in a radio factory
parrot, macaws, a cockatoo. Birds with numbers

on their breasts or tails. Birds in a shooting gallery
and their numbers are up.
78. 23. 43. 12.

One bird must know. The parrot is ducking,
the one behind the bullet hole in the glass.
White bird with a splotch of red on its head.

55 cents an hour, radio parts, bits of distance and boredom
passed along, or not, if flawed.
Who knows what Cornell thought about

desire. Hands across the table were mostly women's.

*

Many items are manufactured to serve as toys, but items produced for other purposes
can also be used as toys. A child may pick up a household item and 'fly' it around
pretending that it is an airplane, or an animal might play with a pinecone by batting
at it, biting it, chasing it, and throwing it up in the air. Some toys are produced
primarily as collector's items and are not intended to be played with.

*

To see into Cornell's "*Roses des vents*" box you must peer through the
glass of twenty-one compass dials or pry them up—pre-museum
days he would sometimes permit a guest to touch—and look through
the holes at the objects underneath: clay marbles, pushpins, spirals,
straw or string, a map of Florida, cutout of the quarter moon, beetle,
sequins, et cetera of all I cannot see in the color plate in my book,

and others, and so forth, and so on, all the "list of illustrations" leaves to oblivion, all that might have been mentioned, et cetera of arrangement, imagination can't help intuiting the hands, arranging for the last time the sundries, ephemera, some long-ago muscle memory actually touching the curve of moon. . . .

*

Gold foil, monarch wing, vermillion shell,
cutout sphinx head, paper spirals intertwined,
could such things, silver twigs, glitter, cork balls,

German maps of the Coral Sea, have begun
to seem self-enclosed? A critic had said
I remembered that there is a war and after that,

*try as I might, I just couldn't find my way back
into Mr. Cornell's world.* White parrot, red splotch
on its head, other splotches, yellow and blue

on a white interior. *How mental it all was*
he wrote to Miss Marianne Moore of a private zoo
he glimpsed each morning and night from the bus,

described its animals and birds and a *profound feeling
of consolation* but not a word about women or the war.
No word of the luckless

parrot, or if red
were the only color
that could wake it up,

no word, the room hot and his shirt wet under the arms,
those women's hands with their nerves and tendons, the 27 bones,
no word of mute temptation or the pleas

from what is merely fragment, shatter, blood.

*

The origin of toys is prehistoric; dolls representing infants, animals, and soldiers, as well as representatives of tools used by adults, are readily found at archaeological sites.

44

*

His letters to women can seem coy, a pose, like a photograph
I saw in *A Pictorial History of Radio*,
the inventor, Dr. DeForest, turning pensively in his fingers

the first three-element electron tube,
not yet "the soul of modern radio," just a clever toy.
No one knew what to do with it yet.

*

He used to ride his bicycle to the beach—I imagine bicycle clips, I
imagine somber trousers and shirt buttoned to the neck, but the world
slips in, lawn mowers, dogs barking, the sun, the blazing sun, though
otherwise I tend to think of him as a man indoors, in basement-
light, kitchen-light, factory-light, or on the streets of New York in the
silvery light of engravings. He collected dried grasses, pieces of glass,
strands of Goldenrod, calling these *examples*, just one of a number
of things that together might accrue in some kind of crazy, seamed
(the lines and juxtapositions of collage are essential), and barely-held-
together . . . whole? Not whole.

*

Bright lips, repetitive motions, hands and sleeves.
A woman ahead of him in the timecard line,
gifts of nothing said each day, each night

the secret lists of her clothes in his diary.
Music at lunch, "the blatant frenzy of jitterbug."
Hands and sleeves, the hands at work

acquiring muscle memory, a kind of secret—arcane—cryptic—
life—
~~so hard to get the diction right.~~
I crossed that out, I can't say why. I can.

Some old-world delicacy under glass—

*

Diction? Hard? What is it with these puns
and hackneyed phallic symbols, spirals and balls,
inventor caressing a tube in his hands,

map of Florida, for heaven's sake, a cockatoo.
Are they mistakes? Or do I now add rockets,
staffs, torpedoes, towers, a snub-nosed warplane

I found in a vintage ad for sale on eBay,
put out by two merged companies that boasted
"A refrigerator and an automobile

GO TO WAR!
Not by ones or twos, but in fleets,
these ocean-jumping Vought-Sikorskys

will be sailing from Nash-Kelvinator assembly lines. . . ."?
Quote Oppenheimer quoting
from the *Bhagavad Gita*

as he watched the rising mushroom cloud?
Shall I?—Nevada, 1945, July 16—
I am become Death, the shatterer of worlds.

*

Who cares if there are phallic symbols in his work?

His "Penny Arcade Portrait of Lauren Bacall"—
she with her downward glance
inside of which a small red wooden ball passes

down a series of concealed glass runways
as if thus he might never have to get to the end of all this
indirection—

the boxes about women are jejune—
they hurt no one, no one, only him—
blue glass—gilt brambles—glass cubes—swan feathers

inhabiting a contraption of inner space—

*

There are sex toys, sex furniture, sex slings, toys sold
in vending machines. Adult toys. Marital aids. Unmarital
aids. Flesh-like materials. Toy boys. Inflatable dolls with orificial mouths.

Glass sex toys. Dildos capable of withstanding extreme temperatures.
Some, with swirls inside, or all blue glass or red,
or knobbed or pebbled beautifully,

are works of art. There's Mr. Blue.
The Studded Wand. The Indigo Intruder.
Then there are Lotus, Ivy, Proteus, Andromeda.

(O daughter of Cassiopeia and Perseus
rescued by—no—from a sea monster.)
String he would, years later, send to a girl, by which he had measured

his penis.
Where are the marbles, constellations, pearl beads, loose red
            and yellow sands?
I turn, lost items, to the asterisk

*

it belongs
in company with all the other toys
left out or left behind

snowflake   ellipsis   candy sprinkle   little star
the tear-spoked asterisk
the Japanese rice star

the sixteen-pointed asterisk
the heavy asterisk
and loneliest of all

the heavy-teardrop-spoked pinwheel asterisk

*

Meanwhile, the parrot is seated—perched—the parrot hunches—
stillness impaired by imaginary velocity, a permanent swerve—on an
object not listed in the "List of Illustrations." It is a twisted rose of a
cork, or it is a piece of driftwood, I can't be sure, but could driftwood
possess so many inward tunnelings—that which causes buoyancy in
a cork? Whatever it is, that thing is the opposite of a sundial, upon
which a bird might deposit its droppings, or safely land, or buzz, or
startle us with its veering wing, a shadow that sun made mortal. What
would Keats say, whose bird was "immortal," "not meant for death,"
whose bird was metaphorical, but real, it was real—

*

*Aircraft factories near the coasts were considered prime targets for enemy air
raids; these plants were often covered with elaborate camouflage scenes intended to
simulate nearby suburbs. In some cases the camouflage was painted on, but these
buildings at Lockheed's Burbank plant and Douglas Aircraft's Santa Monica
factory have canvas-and-wood 'houses' erected on their roofs. Fabric strips were
woven into fake trees, shrubs, and even flower gardens, all for the benefit of enemy
aviators.*

> —online caption of two photos supplied courtesy
> of McDonnell Douglas Corporation and Lockheed
> Corporation, one photo showing a woman in a
> bathing suit clipping the "shrubs"

*

What would you think of this, Miss Moore,
who recommended your friend Elizabeth Bishop revise
"rooster" to "cock"

as a word the more formal and elegant?
He was so polite in his letters.
What would you think of these other

Joseph Cornells? Who knows what they all thought about,
radios or beauty or the war or some woman's hands
or his cock—

do we need to know? Could we simply watch—
not just some lonely wanker, could we watch all of him
from outside a window, if there was a window—

48

O targets in a shooting gallery—
O dried grasses, clump of newspaper, cutouts of birds
placed under shattered glass—

I think there was no window—

*

*The language of any war in the world is killing. I mean the language of war is
victims. I don't like to kill people. I feel sorry they been killed—kids in 9/11.
What will I do? This is the language.*

> —statement by Khalid Shaikh Mohammed at the
> Combatant Status Review Tribunal hearings at
> Guantanamo, March 2007

*

You can see what look like rows of houses
in aerial photographs of the rooftops
of the bomber aircraft factories of Lockheed and Douglas

but they are toys. Each dollhouse has its life-sized
emptiness. Well, no, not really, no. For there are silver crafts inside.
And between the houses there are regular intervals

as any child building a dollhouse town
would by instinct or a simple mimicry allow.
Lawns and shrubs, an almost-loving

attention to detail, so if clouds did not intervene
an enemy bomber pilot, looking down, could imagine
all he couldn't exactly see. Lawn chairs,

barbeques. Bicycles. The war toys.
Courtland mechanical military gun car,
Sky Raiders game, tank bank,

tin fighter plane, a general purpose ammo carrying bag,
the German Tippco Wind-up Tin Toy Bomber Airplane Bomb.
Or maybe he just saw the passed-by look of a sad little town,

maybe he looked down as a homesick child.
Joseph Cornell,
just this once you were not making a toy.

Letter from Mrs. Graham Greene to Her Husband 62 Years after the Blitz

This is not me speaking, this is not you listening. Oh, to open the door of my first Victorian dollhouse and enter, be small enough, lock it behind me. You died . . . I will die . . . perhaps false doors would have suited us. One for the husband, one for the wife, as in the Egyptian tombs, doors of stone outside of which their living left offerings for their dead, supplies for their afterlife. Bread. Beer. Linens. Fowl. The doll-like figurines, tiny furniture, animals, pets, boats, never to be played with, never to serve. Tomb doors never to open: stone slabs carved with hieroglyphics, that figure—woman or man?—seated at a table set with food and drink, its hand reaching out and yet so far away it makes me sad, for I am ninety-eight years old, and blind, and all my dollhouses have been sold lest they become what you and I are: collectors of dust. If I could enter that slab of stone, if I could adjust the crockery on that table, stone food and drink, so real at my fingertips. Barrage bombs, trenches, you and me and the children and the maid being fitted for gas masks. Then you sent us from London. Sixty-two years ago Lucy was sick in the taxi. We had to leave my Victorian snowstorms, clocks and books, the children's toys. Some doors have letter slots, which is one way to speak. Politely begging you: *I would like to come and look after you.* To make you a cake, to bring you blackout shades if you'd only remember to measure the windows. The children were safe with your mother in Crowborough; how willingly I would have left them behind for London. Doodle bugs, Air Raid Warden. Pub windows covered with cardboard so not a gleam would escape. *Doors are the first line of defense against blast and radiation*, the Atomic Energy Commission would intone years later in fear of yet another war. Blast hatch, trap door, bank-vault door, inner and outer doors so the radiation would not reside in us. Alpha, beta, gamma, a lethal hieroglyphics. *Failure to lock the door could be disastrous.* To open the door of my first Victorian dollhouse and enter, door I don't even remember. Long dark evenings of the Blitz, I scraped off its wallpaper and it fell into curls. We were living without you in Oxford rooms by then. Since then I have inventoried 1,500 dollhouses; in unheated rooms I have measured and sketched them, in the dimness of attics and stables of country houses. I should have taken dimensions for false doors, one for each of us, by torch. This is not me. Dollhouse openings, staircases, windows, doors and chimney-pieces, fireplace grates, of these I might say volumes more.

This is not you. In an essay to anyone, you wrote of *a kind of mouse-eye view from behind the stove and dresser*—our London house, bombed open. No doors, no walls. *Oddly enough it leaves one very carefree,* you wrote in a letter, though not to me. What good is open space? Behind blackout curtains I felt something beautiful growing smaller inside. Miniature door with a doorknob made from one of the beads that weighs down a tea cozy. Regency chair that could sit on a matchbox. Winter nights in Bavaria, carpenters made wooden doll furniture, carts and animals, white pine from the forests. I have read that even some coffins had false doors, I have seen dollhouses so exquisite children were only allowed to play with them on Christmas Day, seen dollhouses falling apart, dollhouses donated to children's clinics, *that is to say, suitable for breaking-up as old ships are.* (I wrote that down, in handwriting I barely remember.) It is true I did not allow children to visit my dollhouse museum. Piled blankets, canned goods, Red Cross kit, bottled water, a radio so as to safely enter the afterlife. To whom it may concern: the night seems vast, is the door locked, who left that dollhouse outside in the rain? Doodlebugs, soft rains, a mouse-eye view of the dresser and stove, false doors through which over and over we do not return. The second Gulf war goes on and I am ninety-eight—the children are grown—every last dollhouse sold. Then this letter that in my mind I push through the slot in the door of a house I no longer remember, though I purchased it at an auction and brought it home with me that very night on the bus and the darkness came on fast as if like a child it could not wait.

El Rancho: '50s Subdivision, Phoenix, Arizona

Night with its longing not to be divided from itself:

        night beyond our pall of lights.

How far up is it night up there? Is it OK

        to sleep down here

when sleep is so impersonal we have not

        the language for it, instead we have *bridge* and
            stairs and *fire*

escapes, we have *driveways*, *French windows*

        and *conversation pit* and *rumpus room*,

we have *skylight* to manage the stars

        as they cluster, or flow along as a river

of fluorescence coming around the bend.

        We have numbers, and silence. On cold nights

the stars may look clearer, but that isn't the cold.

        It's the actual brightness of certain stars

visible above the rooftops in winter only.

        Eighteen of the forty-five brightest

rise over streets that keep turning away from themselves,

        stars in a pattern called the Winter Hexagon.

Night, you straight line out of sleep,
        out of the never-snowy, seldom-rainy,
            mostly-clear:

listen to El Rancho here at the edge of the mother

        city, we of the shake roofs and cul-de-sacs

and neighboring spotlights that shine all night.

        El Rancho wants a word

with you, a word *for* you, we have a telegram

        to be sent from the shine, to be delivered

nowhere, light-years away, by a rumor of morning.

Bird Nests over the Gates to Terezín

Nest chambers globular, of mud pellets.
Carried in the mouths

from a shared puddle. Gulp, engulf, a long drink.

Swallows?

A debt is owed to

hinges, latches, metal handles
on each side,

watch hands, mirror fragments,

marbles, cork balls, shell and bone fragments,
crumpled tulle,

doll's forearm, loose red sand.

Gold and blue child's head
attached to a wood block. Hereafter

let all resemblances hide
between the present and the absent.

Let *like* or *as* be
inexplicit memory.

It's not a sky, it's a room.

Nest lined with feathers, sometimes the feathers
curl up around the eggs.

One daily inch, 900-1200 mud pellets in a finished nest.

Mud-dark. *Dark in there*
says a two-year-old son of friends back home
when a toy train disappears in its tunnel

back home,
says it every time, and every time
is right.

Torn paper, working music box, dried leaf fronds,

wood block,
sawdust:

children slept in some of those buildings,
woke in others.

An orchestra played *The Bumble Bee* in the "park" for the
"visitors," 1943.

Quotation marks around child
are no longer extant.

Zdenka Eismannova, she was not a child

when she painted *Early Evening
in Bunk Beds*,

women sitting on their bunks, staring into space,
an in-between,

privacy

now a group emotion, and hazy at that.

Oh nests, you pockets of space. But there are
birds inside you.

Birds keep flying out of you, unswallow
themselves,

network, crisscross, dash—speed—

dart, hurtle, dazzle, flash—ostentation—

joy back in and out again, absence and presence
current, topical, now at this sorrow.

The Pinwheel in Our Neighbors' Flowerbed

Toy of flash and wind,
dear brevity—

the blades revolve, the blades are still.
No way to say the things a pinwheel says and doesn't say.

Two young adults live over there, a man and woman, boyish,
          each of them,
almost like children.

I've never heard them speak a single word.
Has someone cast a spell on them?

Dreamy, she wanders the yard with her watering can.
He turns his bicycle upside down in the grass

the way we used to, feeding handfuls of grass to the turning wheel,
making "popcorn."

It is so young on their side of the chain-link fence.
If I climbed over

I might detect
the soundless tinkle of red and blue and silver

blades moving sadly when the wind resumes.
Over there maybe it isn't sad at all.

Maybe a pinwheel is their little chance offering—
let this or that befall the two of us like rain.

Or possibly they just don't think of it that way,
it's a stick with vanes to scare the rabbits off.

Or it is so familiar they don't even see it anymore,
a toy is part of what they are,

whatever that may be, childless, childlike forever
at least for now, walking around in a yard, never noticing they're
being watched.

The pinwheel turns and glints
and stops, as if the holding still were just as quick.

III

The Small Hours

In the lost and found of lying awake
I have a blue transistor beside me in bed
and a voice like eyeshine coming down
from the moon. I have my glass of milk and my fears
and the window and dark and the dark has Sputnik,
fellow traveler bearing over us its little nigh.
I have this narrator impatient to rise and speak for us all,
including the crickets snoring themselves awake
and the doghouses each with an empty bowl and a doorless door.
There is this silver money clip that lies
on my father's dresser all night, there is money
folded and in the morning counted back into faces
small and comical in the early shift of light.
The moment I turn off my radio and everything gets still
is exactly the moment I can hear the stillness
doesn't exist. Must we, narrator, start talking then?
Our sister's mouth is open and speechless and alone in the languors
of breathing in and out. The puppy sleeps in a box
with a ticking clock. The locked door of our mother and
            father beseeches us
not to wake it up just because I can't sleep again.
And our brother sleeps in a lonely séance
trying to coax him away from his body.
Company, enemy, public, committee, team,
it will take some routine cataclysm to wipe us out.
None of us will hear it
creeping up, if we all say nothing exactly in unison,
if I close my eyes just hard enough, surely this will be as sleep
and sleep will be as travel, each of us
riding into our later lives until each morning
delivers us to a sovereign *we*
of chain-link fences, empty mailboxes,
shoes waiting beside the bed.

Confession of a Luddite

It had been raining, and it would rain.
Without the streetlights tending them
trees turned into a forest,

the houses had fallen back,
I found myself coveting old brass keys
to doors that are lost

and the keys to my old typewriter
for like piano keys,
when you pressed them

something pressed back.
Bill beside me, the two of us walked along
in an elder dark

though an oafish light blared
in a couple of houses powered by the roar
of generators draining the dark

as if it were a basement of water.
But dark was a folk art, dark was a primitive
science composing the very wetness

of bark. No government
could have taken over
so quietly. Without newspapers or stars.

Without the sounds of cars or shoes.
For a moment, nothing needed anything.
Every now and then we came upon candles

deep in houses
and throwing a see-through light,
light that had no argument

with the dark.

Scalp

after chemo

It means leather sheaf. It is not an empty canvas, it is not a lie. It is not a sign of faith or a testament. It is not the truth, but it is true. It hides her skull. It is pale, it has only recently seen the light of day. My own scalp has no answer to hers. I can see in it tiny purple veins. This is something that frightens me. It has me reaching for reference books and diagrams. It is not a trophy or a ticket to anything. It is neither a rune nor a calendar. The hat is too big now. The black and white and olive Harley-Davidson do-rag too loud. It is not quiet, but it makes no noise. It is female but looks masculine like a jaw with a 5 o'clock shadow. Black prickles though the hair was white. Given time enough, it will change, though a map is changeless and thus goes out of style, even a map of outer space. It receives all gaze without acknowledgment, as the moon does. It gives off no light. It has not been anthologized. It is unclaimed territory. The hand finds it occasionally, or its waiting finds the hand. The veins are a rippling. They have miles to go. It is neither waking nor sleep. After a day or two the strangeness ebbs and flows. It is not a blackboard, it is not a screen. It does not address itself to posterity. It justifies no hope, it has no memory, but at certain moments, when the light is careworn, the plain unmannerly style of its beauty may be contemplated if not yet understood.

Book of Invisible Things

And all our gestures go no further than our bodies
And we can reach only as far as our arms go . . .
—Fernando Pessoa

Somewhere trees are vanishing beautifully in a fog. Not on this street.
Trees go on with a silence so deep it is going to be chain-sawed limb
by limb so it disappears from the earth. They're on a hit list early
this morning, wind in their leaves like pages turning in the book of
invisible things. If I could reach far enough outside my body I could
find out where the beginning begins and why at the toes and fingertips
there are so many capillaries bearing so much blood. As for skin, does
the soul come out safely on the other side? In a movie rerun I just
saw, an extraterrestrial revives a dead deer strapped to the hood of a
hunter's car. In the movies a spiritual act takes place from the outside
in, unless the actor is a method actor. This one moves haltingly for
his character's body is borrowed; as he looks on the deer, he wears a
holy strain on the musculature of his face. First its front legs, then
its head wakes up. Limb by limb it struggles back into itself. And it
vanishes, simply by running across the highway into the woods. The
extraterrestrial turns to his human companion and says, *You must be
a very primitive species.* A woman's voice on the radio has gone crackly
with the distance from Pakistan to an early morning in Kalamazoo.
She was raped by decree of a village tribunal she was at the hands not
at the mercy of. She was not, she was *not* to disappear from her body
yet. Having spoken out, she is under house arrest. She is asked by the
interviewer, is she safe and well, is her family supportive, when will
she be given her passport back? Her answers travel out of the mouth
of her translator in an English that is simple and undramatic. Yes.
Yes. Soon. But there is the problem of her real voice coming out
of her real mouth. Voices come to us out of our radios in the early
morning as static. Which is what she is. Which is why her body is
not going anywhere. Wind through leaves sounds like pages turning;
leaves are not voices and do not need throats. Below and above there
are small and large thunders—somebody rolling a garbage can to the
curb, a storm on its way inland from the lake. *If we could hear light,
it would sound like the pitter-patter of individual raindrops falling on a tin
roof* said a scientist on TV last night. Did she want at first to crawl
out of her body? Is it going to rain? Will rain bring the lake down
into the trees? If everyday speech were visible, it might be rain. If
silence were, it might be trees. If only you could look down from
the treetops you would see no houses, no cars in their driveways, no

people. Hard shine of leaves in place of each. Nowhere on earth does anything actually *vanish*, there are lovely synonyms, such as: ash, or shrug.

—NPR Interview with Mukhtar Mai, June 2005

Julie's Mouth

1.

Where are you, how did you get there, is everything closing, is
everything opening, is it light or dark, is it like you imagined, can you
hear John's voice, have you drifted away from your mouth and did you
forget something, a glove or scarf, over here in Kalamazoo?

2.

It feels like she has been dying forever, red Xs spray-painted on trees
all over town, Julie working her way into the big oak tree in front of
my house, a force, a kind of wriggling, arms finding sleeves—

3.

Lately death is not the cutting edge. Instead it's *opportunity, modification,
development, change.* Tell that to one of those trees.

4.

Because every couple of days I take the path fashioned by a neighbor
through years of trees, because they have cut down trees across the
street and dug a hole with a bulldozer, because in the noon hour
silence now has an opening, because there's still a pond over there
somewhere, because water lilies now cover the pond like a living
silence, that neighbor whose name I don't know stops me to say how
turtles lay their eggs on the slope of her woods, and later I read how
the mother digs a pear-shaped nest, lays the eggs, and then, with her
hind legs paddling, buries them.

5.

There are CarePage emails to friends from her husband and family—
not progress but some daily, grieving antonym that isn't a word.

6.

Mouth of dirt opening in the woods at the end of Wilshire in the
month of May, what you open is noise—chainsaw, bulldozer, truck-
music, hammering the same in any language, any ragged opening

7.

—but first the muscles straining to expel the egg—

8.

I fret over the din of construction, that it will frighten the white-throated sparrows away from their haunt near the dentist's office on our side of the woods or will hurry them on their way north to Canada, that the noise will carry from one side of the woods to the other so woods will become a mere idea just as silence is, there really isn't any.

9.

You are nothing like trees, your death is not an x, your name is not carved anywhere that I know of, it is not engraved, though it does appear on the title page, on the spines of your two books, the pressure behind your handwriting is preserved in a note I found in a Mary Poppins book—*here is a (beat up) present for you*—your name is, in your dying, expressing itself (though not to me) some undetectable way—

10.

So hard to stop addressing you. Envelope. Auditorium. Reader. Seashell. Inner ear.

11.

Spring Poem, I called this first. It is deep summer now. I keep wondering what happens, if even in dying you stay exactly yourself. While it was happening, Julie, tulips were coming up.

12.

And there was no one but myself to translate this: I found a strand of silver hair in a book today. A curlicue of handwriting loosened from my scalp.

Y at the End of It

My neighbor Lee is calling her cat home again
in a voice high and sweet
up there in the ether where everything is in question.
Back down inside her the urge
is probably to answer the questions herself—
the name of the cat is both question and answer—
or to save time and actually see the cat
come trotting out of the bushes home.
This time of the morning or this time of the afternoon
the questions are all the same question
and the question in a way is rhetorical:
no answer expected, required, or invited.
The cat is not being issued an RSVP.
This is more command than invitation,
the cat must simply produce: itself.
Now. A cat has no choice but to appear
or not in the backyard of this universe.
I know I've gotten it wrong, maybe she hopes
to persuade him home with her call-note,
like the vireo's at the top of the tallest tree:
Here I am. Where are you?
Ether: the element once believed
to fill all space with itself: that is where
the cat is. That is what the cat is:
what they thought
the stars and planets were composed of.
It is something material
and also: it is absence, about as close
to immateriality as we get. Even when present
it is something over the trees
that might disappear behind clouds,
even when it is curled on the rag rug
by the fireplace and my neighbor is tracing
its backbone as if trailing her hand in water.
It is the moon last night too huge and bright
over the grocery store and it is
streetlights going out when the sky
gets bright enough.
How urgently she requires the cat to come home

is another way for her to answer
her own question: that she doubts
is all over her voice. The name
I can't understand has a "y"
at the end of it, and everything now being queried
—what possible reason, motive, justification for being gone—
hangs in the clear blue sky.

Fifth of July

Yesterday we spoke
      in the voices of Whippersnappers,
           handfuls of noise we hurled
to pavement, just to hear
      the small explosives chorusing like evening
           frogs.
To hear our fingertips grow
      audible.
           Today it is not given to me
to speak anew,
      I am concentrating hard
           on what an unknown
bird is singing now—
      its syrinx is a bow
           drawn back and forth
across the not
      saying anything.
           Not saying words, at least—
though we try hard to bring
      it there, to words,
           or make it visual
by hanging it as if in air,
      the ink vibrations of a sonograph.
           What is a graph anyway
but silence? There:
      the song and countersong of cardinals,
           one in a specific tree,
one some trees
      away. So much I know,
           the rest is out of this world—
so much negotiation
      between birds, who knows,
           maybe between trees.
We mouth such friendless nothings
      when I call my friend today
           then hear under the words
our two unyielding
      presences,
           and it's not at all like the rain

beginning to fall,
     it's just a soundless flickering beneath,
          what she sings and what I sing
make one goddamn
     empty song.
          I need a mile of empty trees,
I need to hear my one unloving
     voice depart from me
          until this lonely radius
dissolves, a rumor
     with a child's spin on it—
          I need to be alone out there.
What she wants, I do not have
     a clue. No wonder on the Fourth
          we spun out noises in the almost-
dark,
     no wonder we couldn't wait
          out dusk to talk the light
of sparklers
     in a truer dark, no wonder smaller
          noises made by light are a kind
of substitution we won't mind—
     fizzle of gunpowder on the air,
          ashworms trying to crawl
right out of their bodies,
     all this begun by the little
          light of a match.

My Parents Contemplate Moving a Last Time

They speak as if they have ten thousand years

To go about recalibrating numbers,
The distance from home to church and shopping, couch to television,

Degree and slant of light in the laundry room.

Light to dark and wall to wall they have been traveling,

Years of back and forth
Between each other's eyes and mouths,

He, asleep in his chair at night, she, riding the dip
She always rides at her end of the couch.

They seem to know time as an ordinary thing

As they sit and procrastinate forever
Over *USA Today* and *The Arizona Republic*,

Half-decaf, melon and toast.

No map of future's day or night, the shallows marked with squiggly lines,
The depths not marked, they are that steep, will guide them;

Nor do they seek the blueprint of a wave.

More coffee, honey? Pass me the Jumble, please.

I watch them contemplate their move so quietly
It resembles just sitting there over breakfast

Talking themselves backwards, toward the smallest house in the
universe—

Address to a Stack of My Journals

. . . it's true that all diaries prefer stillness to commotion.
—*Mary Ruefle*

Finally not much will have happened.
—*Jon Anderson*

How you would have thrived on the moon. Where there is no atmosphere, no wind. Just a jumble of human bootprints forever undisturbed like the diagram of a dance lesson. Just three golf balls, backpacks, plaques and flags. The legs of the lunar module. Mirrors. These would have been enough. All those years traveled by handwriting—I could write for pages and still it was legible, now my handwriting needs a cane. Tucson, Houston, Cincinnati, Cornwall, Suzhou, Kalamazoo. Persistent barking of a dog like the sound of dirt being shoveled. The day I first heard the neighbor calling her cat, her voice getting closer, then farther away. Neither she nor the absence giving up. Friendship seemed fleeting and then like rain it returned. That muffled, mingled talking down by the lake turned out to be a flock of geese. Talk seemed idle even while it was being jotted down. Because it was not happening to me. It was happening the way glints on the water happen to the one on the bridge, looking out. The Cornish butcher shop with its hand-lettered sign, NO ENGLISH BEEF, from the mad cow days. Place and date, no place, no date, absence, the possibility of return versus the mystery of prolonged disappearance. Leaves growing over the addresses. Sometimes I read you from beginning to end, but there is no end, fewer friends maybe, a chickadee calling over and over. My father making do with half-breaths, my mother trundling the heavy garbage can out to the curb at night and a lighter one back to the house in the morning to begin another loop of their life. Loops in my handwriting. What's gone remains. Loops on Tuesdays and Thursdays, the bus to and from Penzance, old women shoppers, their hair dyed black—how hard the day is on their faces.

Lost Continent

I walk past a yard that in the summer is meadow, now in fall a field of ancient stems. An old woman holding a bucket is bent and working at something out of my line of vision, at my approach moving deeper and deeper into the brush. She seems to be deftly maneuvering to be always not-quite-fully-in-sight, the way robins behave in winter, keeping to the woods, flying out from invisibility in the depths of one tree back into invisibility in the depths of another. The thickly falling snow a kind insanity I wish for now, for us to be speechless for once in the same world.

Afterlives

Something is about to pass through. If we stand still
enough. If we sleep

too fitfully.

Early morning's glimmer of steel,
the trees—.

Just to feel it rushing
to stop.

*

Migration is a kind of afterlife—

flight that follows no
particular event.

But by this day last year the white-throated sparrows
had arrived,
successive notes, like silver flecks.

They never stay for long; they're on the way to Canada.

May 5. The absence is too high and thin
to miss.

I saw no Way—the Heavens were stitched—

The smaller birds more comfortable with stars
fly mostly at night.

*

The nearby woods let darkness in and out
so easily
it pools each dusk at every trail head.

And a little dark that stays in us in the daytime
waits.

*

Now that snow is gone we find it:
Alyce Olsen on a Nature Center memorial brick.

Antique handwriting of the chisel,
all you say are names

and numbers
subject to dissolve.

Sunrise and sunset each make a path
one into light one into dark

but that is not where we are going
except maybe for the waxwings

scavenging sideways east and west in flocks,
following the berry line.

*

Deer are the color of trees
when out of mud the dusk makes everything.

Deer are the nothing color at the edge of woods—

three of them poised at the curve
as we are driving by

but as luck would have it
nothing gets hit here tonight,

they don't break from safety as a deer will do

barging out into nothing—a different kind—

*

The river far below
is said to be for birds a low-pitched sound.

The river mangles everything we must have said.

The water is arriving, it is going away.
There are flecks of seed and talk

of sweetness not yet manifested in the brambles.
I don't know what instinct is,

but it gets birds talking up in the trees,
towhees so high you don't ever spot them

singing *drink your tea*
while down below on earth you wonder—

*

will we remember the art
of flinging each other so lightly
we rise, each of us, like many ghosts, not one?

Two deer down the river talked to the water
with their heads down low

just after you and your father let her go.
I don't know, I don't know

what ever comes of this. But they said it anyway.

And when we looked up again, they were gone.

On Not Talking Politics with My Sister

After we tell each other everything on the phone,
so much we say in terms of oppositions,
movies we've seen vs. movies we don't intend to see
no matter what the other's passionate defense,
things we've lately liked vs. things we could not stand,
things that have hurt vs. things to be thrilled about,
do you, too, sense the real words staying out of reach,
that we are tin cans connected by a string,
we are speaking a language of numbers?
Like the joke about prisoners telling each other
the same joke so many times each joke wanes
to a number the joke-teller simply calls out,
and nobody laughs, for the usual reason:
he just can't tell a joke.
I don't mean our talk is an infinite row of zeroes
strung out from you to me and back: there is nothing
infinite about it: we didn't *mean* infinity.
And numbers, at least, may have gotten closer:
add zero to anything and it doesn't change.
You and I, each with so much to say
that when we've been talking an hour and finally agree
to hang up, you go, oh, did you hear about this . . .
as if goodbye were digressive, meandering.
Where will we end up, how late will it be,
I sometimes ask myself, though I can't ask you
without those nonexistent words that might be
a long expensive silence on the phone, complete
with cross winds and a fluttery static
neither of us would know how to answer to.
If I could I'd ask you down an echoey corridor
past our daily joys and sadnesses, to the world's—
a world's, I should say, since we wouldn't know which
world we are even talking about, it won't
hold still—but that we have an unspoken agreement
not to talk *politics*, etymologically plural but taking the singular
as, between you and me, it had better—
a hinterlands I don't want us to find
ourselves wandering the snow-bitten, lonely expanse of.
And yet at each end of the phone, we are

at the beginning of everything we do not say,
can not think to say, could not mean without saying
much too much ever to go back to less trivial silences
from a world we never found a way to talk about.
Still, for an hour you, like me, may be yearning after this—
not pure discourse but the one that doesn't matter,
which ceasing, you and I will once again have begun
to be, without embargo or each other, ourselves.

White-throated Sparrow

Made by trees
tonight, under the care of invisibility, I am trying
to ask my heart, oh why so knotted up? I hear
that it is late and Canada is sweet and still
so many days away, though it silvers
now and then in marsh grass and the leaves.
Darkening present, it is so beautiful
to be out walking
past blackbirds sailing to nowhere on their stalks,
silver thread of a song
about to be pulled through the eye
of a needle if only I stay out here
until it's dark enough.

To a Friend Whose Mother May Be Dying

So it is starting to happen to us middle-aged children,
this dark in the process of growing enormous inside
like an abandoned mine or a geode turned inside out.

We will find out today. They will call us tomorrow.
Or they won't know the results until next year.
Will snow make it different, hearing the news?

We should go about our business as usual.
But what about science? a course of physical therapy? What about rain?
Last night when the power went out, we all kept our windows shut

and the cool in, so why did we all go outside with candles as if at a vigil,
the heat like velvet, hot and soft and terrible?
If you think about it, a heat wave doesn't behave

like a wave, it doesn't move freely and it isn't a greeting.
How much trouble are we in, is this just the beginning?—
heat, tornadoes, hurricanes, not to mention the astronomical

gas prices, glaciers melting and the waters rising on coastal cities foretold
to drown. No wonder sometimes we're struck mute like what lies
at the heart of a telephone pole. Meanwhile, all that thrumming up
    in the wires.

If this is it, what is it, what has it always been?
What about daily exercise? An operation? She looks less distant
if you lose her frame by frame. There she is, doing the dishes.

Walking the dog. Moving so slowly nothing could possibly happen
that wouldn't take forever, take her hand and let her take you back
until science reveals she was moving you gently forward all the while.

You Are Hereby Notified

Having come before the court
these absences—
a lock pried out of a door;
a ledge with nothing on it; nail
holes; eyes and nose
of an empty plug; printer
an open mouth and nothing to say
—the court finds as follows—

or no, first
comes now no sound out of the vent,
no breath of what was heat,
for in the absences the bottom drops
out of the cold
and less and less is said
by rooms upstairs,

away is
not completely quiet or gone,
never is
on earth.

So anyway, they are being
moved—away takes custody of them
—whomever—
you are hereby notified
by a moving van
and a front door unhinged
and a yawn of stairs inside,

this emptying

more about
a family of absences
than the family—where are they?—
whose furniture
is being moved by Two Men and a Truck
(it says on the van),

a they who have already taken the liberty

of moving out of themselves
and are gone
without release or acquittal from you.
As for your claim on pages they left
deliberately blank,

you should read them carefully
and consult your attorney if you have one
other than snow and the fact

it is ten degrees outside.
Notice is hereby given
this was a house
that is a box
unfolded back to flatness
and the truck is a gasp,
two men inside,

a they they
drive away.

Reading the Ice

After the weather has softened its stance
        then hardens again
turning every whim into ridges and gulfs of ice
        and the sidewalk is how you'd imagine
the lunar surface before it was publicly
        translated into so soft a dust,
you must walk with your eyes
        trained down, as if reading the ice.
You must inch cautiously over the miles,
        valleys and hills of a story
that goes so slowly
        you might as well be traveling backwards,
too cold to take your hands
        out of your pockets for balance.
Shallow the ice and almost indecipherable.
        Nevertheless you must go on
reading avidly this morning
        as you walk, everyone goes on reading the ice
to keep from breaking a hip or kneecap
        or the neck, so much at stake
though last night rain hadn't dreamed
        such hills and rills and frozen scree.
It was messy and wet and everyone
        walked with a carelessness you miss,
remembering by chance a missing friend
        walking here less gingerly in another weather
entirely her own. As in a movie
        one of her gestures—lift of the head—
comes back to you, hangs in the air
        as if waiting to be invited back
to a body, to be taking its chances
        once more with the rest of you
over the star-cracks and frozen ruts,
        reading this glacial sway under everything.

Notes

"Pelicans, in a Time of War"—the lines from Bishop quoted in section three can be found in her poem "Florida." The lists of synonyms are courtesy of *Roget*.

"Glacier"—the phrase "deft for so big a ship" is a paraphrase of a comment made by my father (who served on a minesweeper at the end of WWII) about cruise ships.

"The Cold War Special: Tin Litho Dollhouse with Bomb Shelter, 1962"—material in the second section has been culled verbatim from several online chat rooms about dollhouses. The italicized section of somewhat cheery recommendations on bomb shelters comes from nebraskastudies.org/0900/stories/0901_0132.html. The italicized "wild beast or angel" passage in the seventh section of the poem is taken from Joseph Cornell's diary, a slight misquotation from Wallace Fowlie's book *Age of Surrealism*. The phrase "toys of contemplation" comes from M-M. Rabecq-Maillard, *Histoire du Jouet*.

"Flicker"—"Distance is the soul of beauty" is a quote from Simone Weil. Italicized passages are all from Cornell's diary, to be found in *Joseph Cornell's Theater of the Mind: Selected Diaries, Letters, and Files*, ed. Mary Ann Caws.

"Bird Nests over the Gates to Terezín"—"It's not a sky, it's a room" is from Frank O'Hara's poem "Joseph Cornell."

"How We Thought About Toys"—to view photos of the rooftop "suburbs" constructed on top of aircraft factories in California during World War II, see Joel Davidson's essay "Building for War, Preparing for Peace: World War II and the Military-Industrial Complex" in Donald Albrecht's *World War II and the American Dream*. Italicized passages about toys early in the poem are borrowed from an interesting entry on toys from Wikipedia, "the free encyclopedia that anyone can edit." The criticism leveled at Cornell, quoted in Deborah Solomon's *Utopia Parkway: The Life and Work of Joseph Cornell*, is a response by Edward Alden Jewell to a 1943 show including Cornell's work at the Julien Levy Gallery.

"Letter from Mrs. Graham Greene to Her Husband 62 Years after the Blitz"—I owe much of my knowledge of Vivien Greene and her work to Norman Sherry's three-volume biography of Graham Greene and to Vivien Greene's own lovely and eccentric study of dollhouses, *English Dolls' Houses of the Eighteenth and Nineteenth Century.*

"Afterlives"—the italicized line in the poem's second section is from Emily Dickinson.

Some previous titles in the Carnegie Mellon Poetry Series

On the Vanishing of Large Creatures, Susan Hutton

2008
The Grace of Necessity, Samuel Green
After West, James Harms
The Book of Sleep, Eleanor Stanford
Anticipate the Coming Reservoir, John Hoppenthaler
Parable Hunter, Ricardo Pau-Llosa
Convertible Night, Flurry of Stones, Dzvinia Orlowsky

2009
Divine Margins, Peter Cooley
Cultural Studies, Kevin A. Gonzalez
Cave of the Yellow Volkswagen, Maureen Seaton
Group Portrait from Hell, David Schloss
Birdwatching in Wartime, Jeffery Thomson
Dear Apocalypse, K. A. Hays
Warhol-o-rama, Peter Oresick

2010
Admission, Jerry Williams
The Other Life: Selected Poems, Herbert Scott
In the Land We Imagined Ourselves, Jonathan Johnson
The Diminishing House, Nicky Beer
Selected Early Poems: 1958-1983, Greg Kuzma
Say Sand, Daniel Coudriet
A World Remembered, T. Alan Broughton
Knock Knock, Heather Hartley

2011
Copperhead, Rachel Richardson
Working in Flour, Jeffrey Friedman
Oz, Nancy Eimers
The Politics, Benjamin Paloff
Having a Little Talk with Capital P Poetry, Jim Daniels
Scorpio Rising: Selected Poems, Richard Katrovas